HAWAII

Waialua Falls on the island of Maui. Previous page shows memorial at Pearl Harbor dedicated to Navy men killed on December 7, 1941.

HAWAII

BY ALMA E. THOENE

illustrated with photographs

FRANKLIN WATTS, INC.
575 Lexington Avenue • New York, N.Y. 10022

Photographs courtesy of: Dole Pineapple Company, page 34; Hawaii Visitor's Bureau, pages 16, 19, 20, 27 top left; State of Hawaii, opp. page 1, page 31; all others by Robert Wenkam, photographer, Honolulu, Hawaii. Cover photograph (courtesy United Air Lines) shows Kona Coast on island of Hawaii.

Library of Congress Catalog Card Number: 68-10188
Printed in the United States of America
1 2 3 4 5

This book is dedicated to the young people of Hawaii in the hope that it will help them to take pride in their state and, through the spirit of *aloha*, bring understanding and goodwill between our nation and the people of the Pacific Rim.

For further information the books and periodicals listed in the bibliography will be of inestimable value to the reader. Other sources of knowledge are the various current governmental, private industrial, and organizational reports from the libraries of Hawaii's leading newspapers, the *Honolulu Advertiser* and the *Honolulu Star-Bulletin*, from the Bishop Museum, the Hawaiian Historical Society, and the Public Library.

To the many people who assisted in checking the various areas of the manuscript and shared information via the telephone, I am profoundly grateful. Among these kind and generous individuals are Dr. Deal Crooker, director, Division of School and Library Services of Grolier International, Inc., in Honolulu; Mr. Doroteo M. Collado, Sr., president of the Philippine-American Good Will Foundation; Mr. Kenji Ego, chief of the Fish Bureau, Fish and Game Division, Department of Agriculture of Hawaii; Mrs. Flora K. Hayes, member of the Territorial Legislature for many years; Dr. Andrew W. Lind, professor of sociology at the University of Hawaii and author of many books and articles on race relations in Hawaii; Mrs. Mary K. Pukui, retired specialist in Hawaiiana at the Bishop Museum; Mr. Robert C. Schmitt, state statistician assigned to the Department of Planning and Economic Development; Dr. F. Wallrabenstein, statistician in the State Department of Agriculture in charge of the Crop and Livestock Reporting Service and federal statistician in the same area; and Mr. David Woodside, chief of the Game Bureau of the State Department of Agriculture. The gracious cooperation of members of the State Department of Education (including Mrs. Jean Aten, Pauoa School librarian), the United States Information Agency, the Lieutenant Governor's office, The Hawaiian Pineapple Research, Incorporated, the State Board of Health, and the East-West Center office at the University of Hawaii is very much appreciated also.

Contents

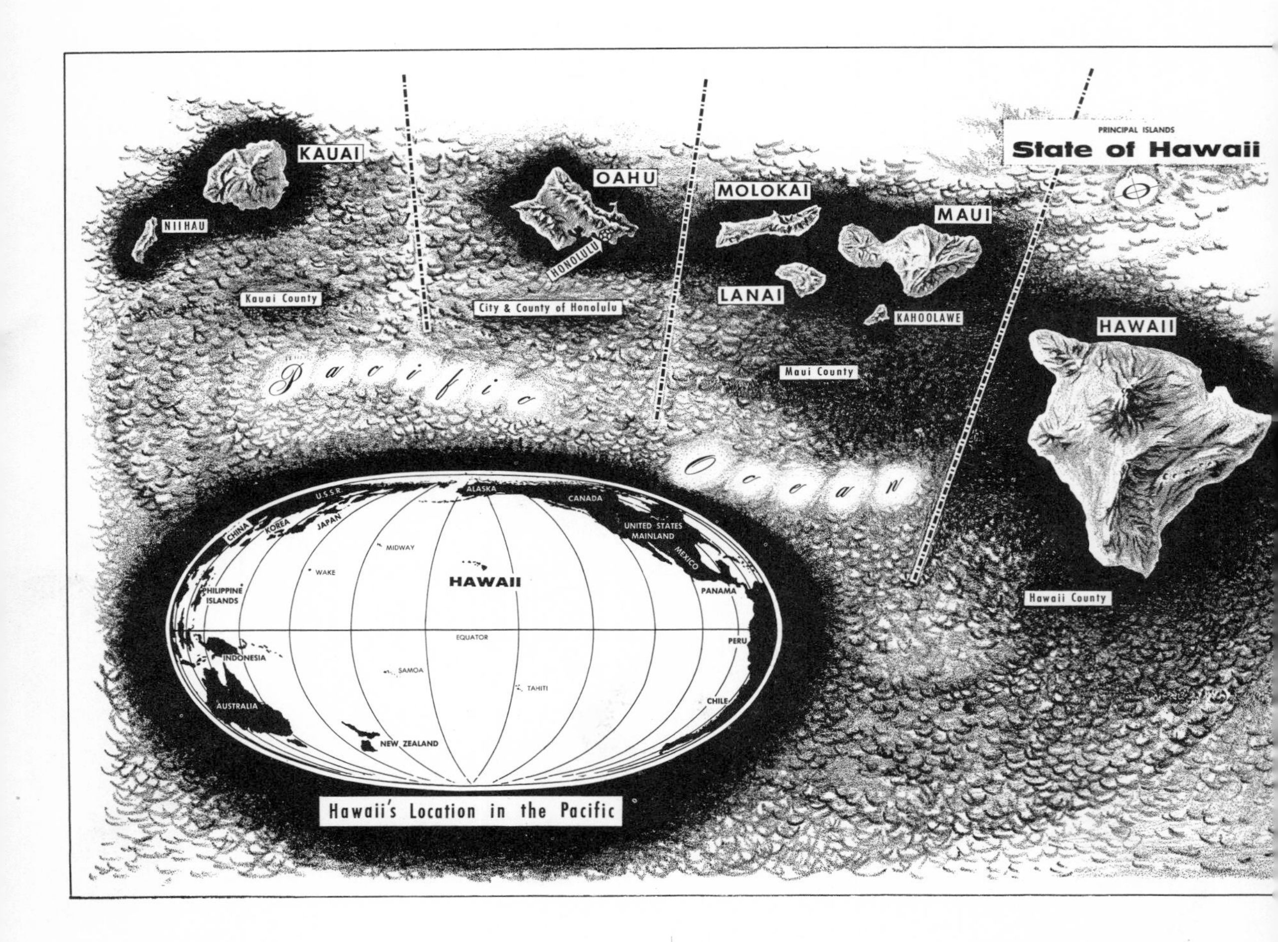

Hawaii's Location in the Pacific

CROSSROADS OF THE PACIFIC

HAWAII is the youngest of the fifty states. It was admitted to the Union on August 21, 1959. However, being the newest member is only one of the many ways in which Hawaii differs from her sister states.

Hawaii is the only state which cannot be reached by land travel. This is because Hawaii is an archipelago, a cluster of islands, in the Pacific Ocean. About fifteen hundred miles long, this group of islands is some twenty-one hundred miles west-southwest of San Francisco. To reach the fiftieth state takes about four and a half days by steamship from San Francisco, or about five hours by jet plane.

Because of its location, Hawaii is often called the Crossroads of the Pacific, as well as the Gateway to the East and the Gateway to the United States. It is a convenient stopover for planes and ships from countries bordering the Pacific. Its location also makes it an important military area for the United States. During World War II the Hawaiian Islands became a tremendous military base, with such centers as Pearl Harbor and Hickam Air Force Base. Today the state continues to play a major role in our country's defense. And as greater interest centers in the Asian countries, Hawaii becomes ever more important as a cultural and economic bridge between the West and the Orient.

Hawaii is the southernmost state in the country. Its balmy subtropical weather is due to the fact that it lies in the temperate zone and is cooled by prevailing northeast trade winds. The climate, with its average year-round temperature of 75 degrees, as well as the rare beauty of the green mountains, clear blue sky, white beaches, exotic flowers, and colorful birds, has earned Hawaii another name — Paradise of the Pacific. Thousands of visitors come each year from the mainland and other countries to enjoy this beautiful land.

Many people live along the shore and in the valleys on the island of Oahu.

Another distinction draws visitors to Hawaii, too — the well-known warmth and friendliness of the people. Hawaii's population — a mixture of many peoples — lives together in peace and harmony. Because of this, Hawaii is called by yet another name — Melting Pot of the Pacific. Hawaii's race relations have long been a proud example of how people can live together peacefully and happily.

The state of Hawaii includes 124 islands. The eight largest are Hawaii, Maui, Oahu, Kauai, Molokai, Lanai, Niihau, and Kahoolawe. With a land area of 6,424 square miles, Hawaii is the fourth smallest state in the nation. Only Connecticut, Delaware, and Rhode Island are smaller. However, Hawaii has the fourth longest coastline in the country — 750 miles. The eight main islands have 99.9 per cent of the land, and the island of Hawaii itself accounts for 62.7 per cent.

Hawaii also has the largest city in the United States, not in population but in total area. The capital city of Honolulu on the island of Oahu actually stretches almost fourteen hundred miles northeast to Kure Island and includes the islands of Nihoa, Necker, French Frigate Shoal, Laysan, Lisianski, Pearl, and Hermes Reef.

Although the Hawaiian Islands are as modern as any of the other forty-nine states, it is the only state in the Union in which the governor lives in the former home of a queen and the legislature meets in what was once a royal palace.

Snow on Mauna Kea cinder cones

GEOGRAPHY OF THE ISLAND STATE

According to a Polynesian tale, the islands of Hawaii were created by a magic fishhook. Maui, a young boy, had visited the Underworld and obtained a human jawbone from one of his ancestors in order to make the hook. He persuaded his older brothers to take him fishing. When the canoe was in deep waters, he baited the hook with a sacred bird and threw it down to the Old-Man-at-the-Bottom-of-the-Sea. Suddenly the line grew taut. Maui and his brothers pulled and tugged until they were near exhaustion. At last, a strange catch appeared above the water. It was not a fish at all. Instead, Maui had pulled from the ocean a beautiful green island, complete with lush valleys, glistening beaches, and bright-colored flowers, and crowned with rainbow mists.

Actually, the Hawaiian Islands were created not by a magic fish-hook but by active volcanoes. They were built up from the ocean floor by eruptions over a long, long period of time. The islands of Hawaii are really the tops of a chain of mountains, beginning with Kure in the northernmost part of the state and continuing down to Hawaii itself, the highest and the youngest.

The island of Hawaii, 4,030 square miles, is also the largest. It contains both the highest mountain in the state and the only active volcanoes. Mauna Kea, a dormant volcano, is actually the highest mountain in the world. It is 13,784 feet above sea level, but it drops

Cinder cones inside Haleakala Crater

some 18,000 feet to the ocean floor for a total height of almost 32,000 feet. Snow covers its peaks during the winter months. The active volcanoes are on Mauna Loa, which rises 13,680 feet above sea level. Periodically the craters of Mauna Loa flare up and spill out boiling lava, which makes its way to the sea. The 1955 eruption continued off and on for three months and caused the greatest property damage in the history of the islands.

The island of Maui, next largest with 728 square miles, has the world's largest extinct volcanic crater. It is on top of a mountain called Haleakala, or House of the Sun, which is 10,025 feet high. The crater measures 33 square miles, and has been extinct since about 1750. Visitors can drive a car on a well-paved road right to the crater, and the more adventurous ones can ride a horse inside the crater around the cones, one of which is taller than the Empire State Building in New York City.

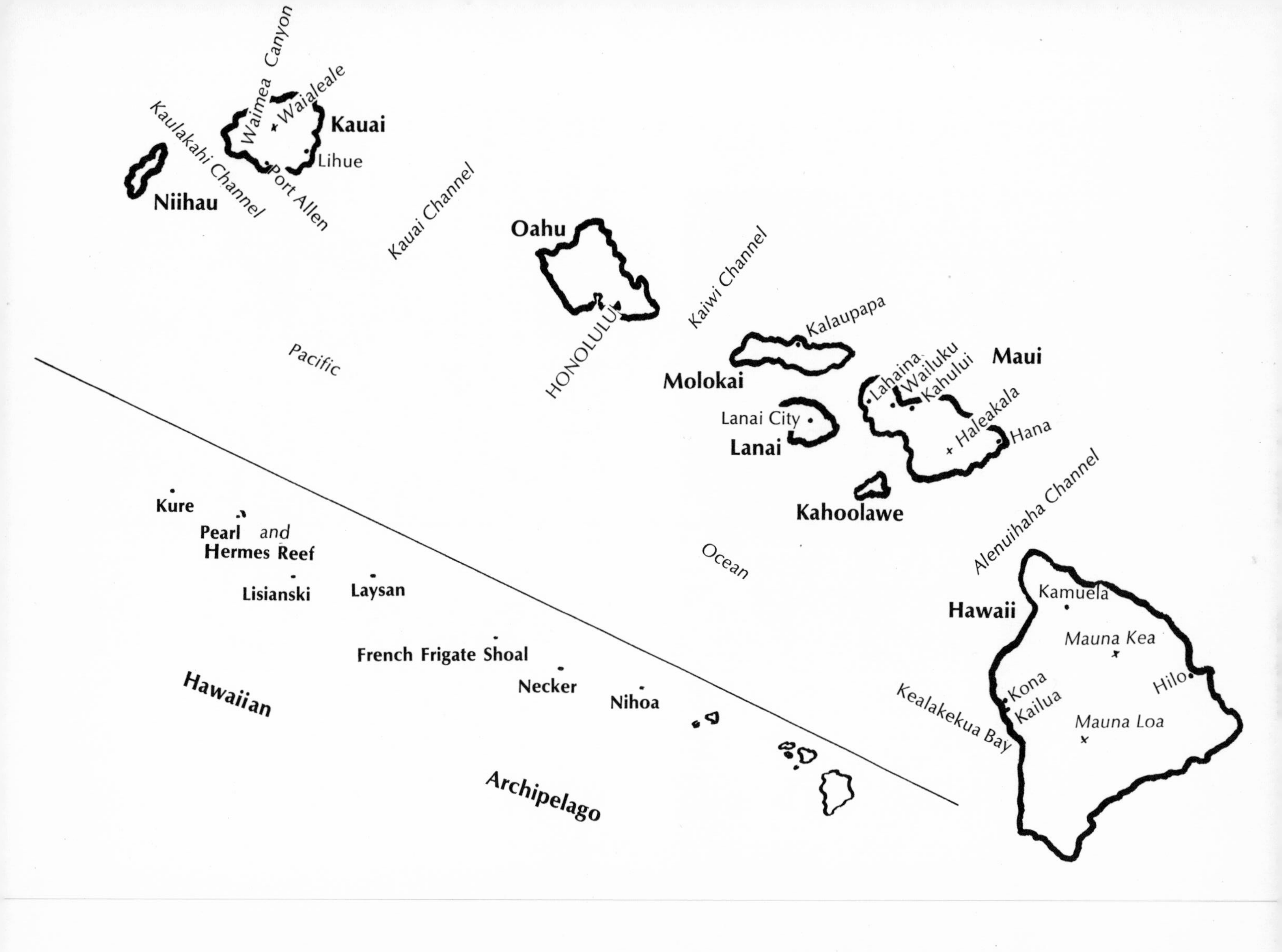

Waimea Canyon
Waialeale
Kauai
Lihue
Kaulakahi Channel
Port Allen
Niihau
Kauai Channel
Oahu
HONOLULU
Kaiwi Channel
Pacific
Kalaupapa
Molokai
Maui
Lahaina
Wailuku
Kahului
Lanai City
Lanai
Haleakala
Hana
Kahoolawe
Alenuihaha Channel
Ocean
Kure
Pearl and Hermes Reef
Lisianski
Laysan
French Frigate Shoal
Necker
Nihoa
Hawaiian
Archipelago
Hawaii
Kamuela
Mauna Kea
Kona
Kailua
Hilo
Mauna Loa
Kealakekua Bay

Other dormant volcanoes are Punchbowl, Koko Head, and Diamond Head on Oahu. Oahu, area 604 square miles, also has three natural harbors: Pearl Harbor, the largest and most important; Honolulu Harbor, the main civilian harbor in the state and a haven for ships crossing the Pacific; and Kaneohe Bay, used chiefly for small fishing and pleasure crafts. Like the other islands, Oahu has a shoreline protected by coral reefs. Ships can enter only where there is a natural or man-made channel.

Kauai, 555 square miles, is the fourth largest island and geologically the oldest of the eight main islands. It is actually one central mountain mass. Erosion has cut heavily into the mountains, leaving deep valleys and canyons. The most spectacular is Waimea Canyon. Its awe-inspiring beauty can be compared to the Grand Canyon on a smaller scale. On the southeastern shore of Kauai are the Barking Sands, so-called because when the wind blows the dry sand it makes a sound like a dog barking.

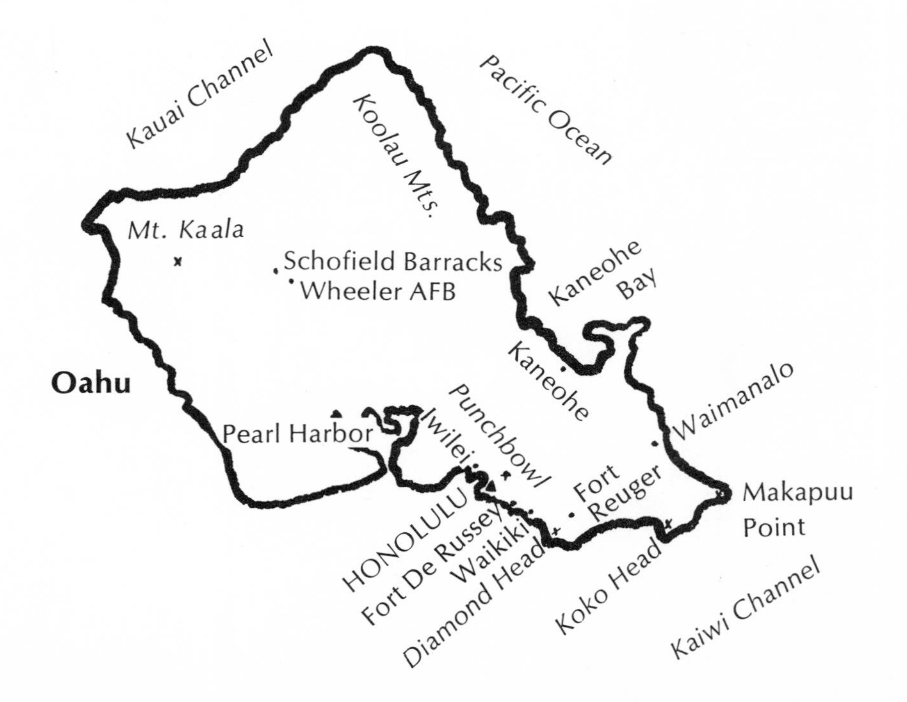

Waimea Canyon

Molokai, 260 square miles, has two extinct volcanoes. Rugged cliffs and valleys cover most of the eastern side. In the north-central area is the leper colony of Kalaupapa.

Lanai, 141 square miles, and Niihau, 72 square miles, are privately owned and devoted to the raising of pineapples and cattle respectively.

Kahoolawe, smallest of the main islands with its 45 square miles, is dry and uninhabited. Because it is leased to the federal government as a target area for military ships and planes, it is also called Target Island.

Hawaii's weather is balmy, and the northeast trade winds bring a great deal of moisture to the islands. In fact, Waialeale, a mile-high peak on Kauai, is one of the two wettest spots in the world (the other is in India). Waialeale gets about 476 inches of rain each year. Hilo, on the island of Hawaii, is the rainiest city in the United States, with an annual rainfall of 141 inches.

There are small streams only and no large lakes in the state. Water conservation is therefore very important, and in some areas people must depend upon the rainfall for water. Sugar plantations have been responsible for much research and development of mountain waters.

These girls represent the many racial groups in Hawaii.

THE MELTING POT–HAWAII'S PEOPLE

THE state of Hawaii has a population of 756,000, over half of whom are Oriental. The islands are a melting pot of Hawaiians, Japanese, Caucasians, Chinese, Filipinos, Koreans, Negroes, and others. Nearly 90 per cent of the people are American-born. The island of Oahu is the most populous: 80 per cent of the state's people live there. Hawaii ranks second, Maui third.

The most striking thing about the population of the islands is the peaceful way in which all races live together. Tourists are immediately impressed by the warmth and friendliness of the people, symbolized in the word *aloha*, which is used for both hello and good-bye and expresses love or affection. One of Hawaii's nicknames is the Aloha State.

How has Hawaii been able to achieve such harmony among its people? The story begins with the first Hawaiians, the original settlers. There are many theories about where these settlers came from, but the most popular one is that they were a branch of the Polynesian people in southeast Asia. The name Hawaii comes from Hawaiki, traditional homeland of the Polynesians. Skillful navigators, these first settlers sailed from Tahiti, twenty-five hundred miles south of Hawaii, in about A.D. 750. In their large double canoes they brought food and tools from their former homes, using the stars as guides. The Hawaiians were ruled by chiefs, called *alii*, who were tall and athletic. They were a religious people, skilled in astronomy, herb medicine, anatomy, weaving, music, and other arts. Despite the fact that they had no metals, they had developed a highly refined civilization by the time the first white men arrived.

Although there are only about 10,000 pure-blooded Hawaiians in the state today, there were probably 300,000 in 1778. In that year, on January 18, Captain James Cook, a British explorer, became the first white man to discover Hawaii, which he called the Sandwich Islands after his employer, the Earl of Sandwich. The people were friendly and regarded Cook as some kind of god. However, the following year he was killed in a battle between his men and the Hawaiians at Kealakekua Bay on the island of Hawaii.

Between 1792 and 1794 another British explorer, Captain Vancouver, arrived in Hawaii, and he was soon followed by more adventurers. From 1819 to 1880 seamen from the whaling ships brought useful animals and plants to the islands, but they also brought disease, guns, and whiskey. As a result, the number of Hawaiians began to drop; by 1823 it had fallen to 130,000. King Kamehameha I, who had tried to stop the corruption of his people, died in 1819. He was replaced by his son Liholiho as Kamehameha II, and Queen Kaahumanu as the *kuhina-nui*, or prime minister.

Kaahumanu, who destroyed the tabu system, was converted to Christianity by the missionaries who arrived from England on March 13, 1820. They built churches and schools, printed books, and started the little kingdom on the road to Western civilization.

After the missionaries were established, more and more white men came to the islands. French Catholics arrived in 1840; Scots, Scandinavians, and Germans from 1881 to 1885. Many became overseers on the plantations. The Portuguese, the largest single group of immigrants, arrived from 1878 to 1887 and stayed the longest on the plantations. Poles came in 1897 and 1898, and Russians from 1909 to 1912. Most of the immigrants came to Hawaii to work on the plantations. After their contracts expired, many remained in agriculture; others returned to their homelands. Today about 290,000 Caucasians live in the islands.

In 1802 the first Chinese immigrant came to Hawaii and set up a sugar mill at Wailuku on Maui. But it was not until 1855 that the first group of Chinese came to work on the sugar plantations. By 1898 there were 46,000 Chinese laborers in the islands. However, the Chinese were not happy on the plantations and soon began to move into the cities of Honolulu and Hilo, where they became tailors, cooks, bakers, storekeepers, and restaurant owners. Many

Hilo, with Mauna Kea in the distance

Hawaiian children at play

entered teaching, law, engineering, medicine, and dentistry. As a result, a number of Hawaii's foremost leaders are of Chinese ancestry. About 40,000 Chinese live there today.

In 1881 King Kalakaua visited Japan to recruit workers for the sugar plantations. Although he was unsuccessful, Japanese laborers began to arrive in 1886 due to crop failures in their own country. Out of the 180,000 Japanese who came to Hawaii, over half returned to Japan. The deep sense of Japanese family pride added another element to the growing melting pot of Hawaii. These people, too, became dissatisfied with plantation life, and in 1904 they began to enter the cities. They became carpenters, merchants, fishermen, gardeners, and coffee farmers. During World War II many second-generation Japanese, or Nisei as they were called, became members of the famed 100th Battalion and 442nd Regiment in Europe. After the war they entered politics, medicine, education, law, and business. Today over 200,000 Hawaiian citizens are of Japanese ancestry.

Other groups were brought to Hawaii to work on the plantations: Puerto Ricans (3,000 in 1900), Negroes (a few hundred in 1900), Koreans (several thousand in 1904), and Filipinos. From 1910 to 1932, 100,000 Filipinos came to the islands. Half of them returned to the Philippines or emigrated to California by 1940. Those who stayed gradually entered the business and social life. They have sponsored such groups as the Filipino-American Good Will Week Committee, which helps to promote better relationships between the two countries. Filipinos, a hardworking people who enjoy life, now number more than 73,000 in Hawaii.

As each group came to Hawaii, it brought its own customs and cultures, which have been adapted to life in the islands. Through intermarriage and education the groups have largely merged into one. Although the people have many differing backgrounds and customs, they maintain a feeling of respect and tolerance for the individual. They pride themselves on the spirit of *aloha* that pervades every corner of the state.

King Kamehameha I

HISTORY AND GOVERNMENT

THE governor of Hawaii lives in the former home of a queen. The legislature meets in what was once a royal palace. Washington Place is the governor's home, and it originally belonged to the last of Hawaii's queens, Liliuokalani. The legislature sits in Iolani Palace, built in 1882 by King Kalakaua. When the new state building is finished, however, the palace will be restored to its original splendor as a museum.

Hawaii began its long journey from kingdom to statehood in 1795, when Kamehamaha I united the islands under his rule and appointed a governor for each one. The king and his chiefs owned all the land, but the people were allowed to cultivate small areas. Kamehamaha encouraged agriculture and industry, and was generally friendly to foreigners although he fought against attempts to colonize his kingdom.

Before Kamehameha's death in 1819 he created the office of prime minister. Queen Kaahumanu was the first to hold the position. She abolished discrimination against women and destroyed all idols and temples before her death in 1832.

After the American missionaries arrived in 1820, Kamehameha's successor, Liholiho, Queen Kaahumanu, and their followers became pupils in the mission schools and encouraged the people to do likewise.

The missionaries were responsible for giving the Hawaiians a written language. Hawaiian is a Polynesian dialect, as is Tahitian or Samoan. There are twelve letters in the alphabet — *a, e, h, i, k, l, m, n, o, p, u,* and *w*. The letters are pronounced much the same as in English except for the *w*. If followed by *a, o,* or *u,* the letter has a *w* sound, as in Waikiki. If preceded by *i* or *e,* it is pronounced as a *v*, as in Ewa (*e*-vah). Every syllable and word ends in a vowel and each vowel is pronounced separately. The apostrophe, which represents the guttural break, is an important part of the language because it can change the meaning of a word — *i'a* means *fish*; *ia* means *he, she, it,* or *this*. On January 7, 1822, the *palapala* became the first book printed in Hawaiian. It contained the alphabet, some words, and a few simple sentences.

Kamehameha III, who was crowned in 1825, approved the first written constitution in 1840. He abolished old feudal systems and established a limited monarchy with a legislature and a judiciary system. He also authorized the Great Mahele, which divided the land among king, government, and people.

In 1843 England forced Kamehameha to cede his country to the British government. The king asked the President of the United States, John Tyler, for help. Through the President's intervention Hawaii was restored to its status as an independent nation.

During the following years the royal leaders tried to improve the life of their people. Kamehameha IV, who was crowned in 1854, tried to better the health standards. He obtained funds to construct the Queen's Hospital, which was completed in 1860. King Lunalilo was the first royal ruler to be elected by the people. After his death in 1874 he left his estate to the poor and destitute. The Lunalilo Home for Aged Hawaiians is a monument to his concern. In 1874 Kalakaua became Hawaii's last king. He visited the United States and in 1876 signed a Reciprocity Treaty providing for free trade between the two nations. The United States renewed the treaty in 1887 and received permission to use Pearl Harbor as a naval station. Kalakaua died in San Francisco in 1891.

Hawaii's last royal ruler and last queen was Liliuokalani, a well-

Statue of King Kamehameha I is draped with leis in honor of his birthday.

educated monarch who became famous for her musical compositions, among them the song "Aloha Oe." When she tried to install a new constitution that would give the monarch greater powers, the result was the Revolution of 1893. A provisional protectorate government was formed with Sanford B. Dole as president. Liliuokalani appealed to President Grover Cleveland for help. He sent an investigator and the provisional government fell. A new constitution was drawn up, and the Republic of Hawaii was proclaimed on July 4, 1894. After an abortive attempt to restore the monarchy Liliuokalani was imprisoned, but she renounced all rights to the throne on January 4, 1895. Until her death in 1917 she continued to help the Hawaiian people.

Inscription on the Great Seal of the State of Hawaii means: "The life of the land is preserved by righteousness."

The leaders of the republic asked for annexation to the United States after President William McKinley had been inaugurated. On August 12, 1898, formal ceremonies were held at Iolani Palace, and the Hawaiian flag (which is the state flag today) was replaced by the Stars and Stripes. The constitution was allowed to continue as the main law so long as it did not conflict with the Constitution of the United States.

In April, 1900, Congress passed the Organic Act, which established a territorial form of government in Hawaii. Sanford B. Dole was appointed the first governor of the Territory of Hawaii, and the first territorial legislature met on February 26, 1901. After the first elections three political parties emerged — Republican, Democratic, and Home Rule. The Home Rulers won the election, but in 1902 Prince Kuhio Kalanianaole, a Republican, was elected Hawaiian delegate to the United States Congress, a post he held until his death in 1922.

From 1900 until World War II agriculture and the economy began to flourish. County governments were set up, as well as the city government of Honolulu. However, after December 7, 1941, with the United States' entrance into World War II, martial law was declared and the government was turned over to Lieutenant General Walter D. Short. A rigid blackout, a curfew, and gasoline rationing went into effect. People were fingerprinted, identification cards were issued, and typhoid and smallpox shots were administered.

Although the people of Hawaii accepted martial law as a necessity during the first months of the war, they became increasingly restless under the restrictions as the fighting progressed. Through the efforts of Governor I. M. Stainback and others, martial law was partially lifted in March, 1943, and ended in October, 1944.

After the war the drive for statehood began in earnest. To be sure, many Hawaiians had long battled for acceptance as a state. As early as 1853 King Kamehameha III had explored the possibilities of statehood. On January 8, 1896, General George Spaulding, congressman from Michigan, had introduced a resolution calling for

John A. Burns in the governor's office in Iolani Palace. Note state flag and seal.

the admission of Hawaii as a state. But many leaders objected on the grounds that the mixed population of the islands was not ready for the responsibilities of statehood. This objection continued to be a forceful one until the actual admission of Hawaii.

Others kept urging statehood: W. R. Farrington, later governor of the Territory; Prince Kuhio, who introduced a statehood bill in Congress in 1919; Victor Houston, delegate to Congress; Samuel W. King, delegate and later governor; and Joseph R. Farrington, a delegate who sponsored statehood legislation at home. Finally a Constitutional Convention was called in 1950. The bill for Hawaiian statehood was approved by the legislature and ratified by the voters at the next general election.

Although certain groups both in Hawaii and on the mainland still voiced their objections, the Eighty-sixth Congress granted statehood to Hawaii on March 12, 1959. At a general election the people of Hawaii voted in its favor by 131,000 to 7,000, electing William F. Quinn, Republican, as governor. (John A. Burns, Democrat, was elected governor in 1962.) President Eisenhower signed the Statehood Proclamation on August 21, 1959, and Hawaii officially became the fiftieth state in the Union.

The state constitution of Hawaii provides for a senate of twenty-five members elected for four years, and a house of representatives of fifty-one members elected for two years. It divides the state into four counties: Hawaii, Maui, Honolulu, and Kauai. Honolulu is governed by a city charter in effect since 1959, which provides for a mayor and city council. Each of the other counties is governed by a board of supervisors. All United States citizens over twenty may vote, provided they have lived at least twelve months in the state and three months in their district.

Ohia lehua trees

PLANT AND ANIMAL LIFE

To the visitor the islands of Hawaii may seem to be one huge tropical garden. More than three hundred kinds of flowering plants and three hundred kinds of trees, as well as ferns, lichens, and fungi, give the state one of the greatest selections of plant life in the world.

The rainfall over the mountains results in lush vegetation on the windward sides and more sparse plant growth on the leeward sides. The deep valleys are verdant the year round with such fruit trees as guavas, mountain apples, star fruit, bananas, avocados, mangoes, and others. Beautiful tropical plants, such as wild orchids, tree fern, ginger, ti leaf, and bird-of-paradise, are a colorful delight to the traveler. Hibiscus, the state flower, appears in many varieties.

Tall coconut palms grow along the seashore and on the plains, along with hala, whose thorny leaves are woven into mats, bags, and hats; kamani nut, one of the few leaf-shedding trees in Hawaii; and the feathery algarrobas. Bursting with color are such trees as the poinciana, jacaranda, African tulip, plumeria, and vines and shrubs such as bougainvillea, star jasmine, cup-of-gold, and poinsettia.

The early Hawaiians were skilled in the use of herbs for medicine, and many of their plant cures are still used today. The bruised leaves of hiiloa are used as a poultice; noni, laukahi, and poha leaves are used to cure boils; kokea or sugarcane for colds; popolu berries as a tonic; and ohia bark for sore throats.

Of Hawaii's 1,723 types of seed plants, almost 95 per cent have developed in the islands and are dependent upon special conditions. Some are so specialized that they are found only in one spot. For example, the silversword grows only on the slopes of Haleakala on Maui.

About 272 plant species are said to have been carried to Hawaii by storms, ocean currents, and birds. It took many ages for the lava which erupted from the volcanoes to cool and become pulverized by sun, wind, and rain in order to support vegetation. But when the seeds arrived, they were able to thrive in the black and red mountain soil, the claylike adobe soil of the valleys, and the sandy soil of the beaches and plains.

By the time the first Hawaiians came to settle, the mountains and valleys bloomed with forests of kou and acacia trees, which are used for tanning and making furniture; with sandalwood, a fragrant wood used in ornamental carving; and fern trees. The Hawaiians brought with them fifty varieties of bananas; the coco palm; hala, or pandanus tree; the hau, which has a light wood used by the

Hala, or pandanus, trees

Some of Hawaii's plants include the hibiscus (top left); the ape-ape plant with tree ferns (top right); hanging heleconia blossoms (bottom left); and the silversword (bottom right).

Hawaiians in their canoes; the kukui, or candlenut tree, whose oil was used in torchlights. The inner bark of the paper mulberry was pounded into *tapa* cloth; sugarcane, sweet potato, and taro gave food; and the broad leaves of the ti plants provided skirts, table coverings, and food wrappings.

After Captain Cook's arrival many plants were brought to Hawaii as gifts to the kings and queens. In this way, pineapple from the West Indies, coffee from East Africa and Brazil, as well as macadamia nuts, orchids, and anthurium arrived and eventually became important items in the Hawaiian economy.

Although most of Hawaii's plants are native to the region, most of the state's animals are not. The early Polynesians brought chickens (*moa*), pigs (*puaa*), and dogs (*ilio*). They found only bats and seals. Bats still fly along the beaches on the island of Hawaii in the evenings, and they help to control mosquitoes and other insects. Hawaiian seals, which grow to five hundred pounds, were practically wiped out during whaling days because of their oil. However, they are now increasing in number because they are protected by strict conservation laws.

Captain Cook brought goats, rats, and lizards to the islands, and Captain Vancouver contributed sheep and horses. Hawaiians came to pride themselves on their excellent horsemanship.

The emperor of Japan gave a gift of Axis deer to Hawaii in 1867. Today the deer flourish on the islands of Molokai, Lanai, and Maui. Blacktail deer are found on Kauai, and pronghorn antelope roam Lanai. These animals, as well as wild pigs, goats, sheep, and cattle, are protected by the Division of Fish and Game.

In 1883 the mongoose, a weasel-like animal, was imported from India to catch rats in the cane fields. But the mongoose proved ineffective as a rat-catcher and became a nuisance to poultry farms and wild birds. European hares and domestic cats were also brought in on some of the first vessels. Cats now run wild on all the islands and are serious threats to ground-nesting birds.

A few wallabies, a kind of kangaroo, were brought into Hawaii

This Hawaiian forest has ohia lehua trees, banana trees, tree ferns, anthuriums, and other plants.

in 1916, but they escaped into the Kalihi Valley on Oahu. Occasionally someone spots a wallaby as it roams about the island woodlands.

One animal that Hawaii does not have is the snake. They are forbidden by law, even for exhibition purposes. The baggage and freight inspectors of the State Board of Agriculture and Forestry are charged with the duty of keeping Hawaii snake-free. If one of the reptiles is found, it is immediately put to death. The islands do have a few reptiles, however, among them the little gecko and skink lizards, which are harmless and help to keep homes free of mosquitoes. Hawaii also has bullfrogs and the giant bufo toad from South America.

There are 3,700 kinds of native insects, including weevils, moths, bees, beetles, flies, and wasps. Grasshoppers, monarch butterflies, and mosquitoes have found their way to the islands. The government helps to control the spread of plant and animal diseases coming from outside the state by a system of quarantine on incoming species.

Hawaii's produce includes taro, cabbages, avocados, macadamia nuts, soy beans, coffee, and yams.

The nene

The official bird of the fiftieth state is the Hawaiian nene goose. A century ago this large bird was found in great numbers on the islands of Hawaii and Maui. However, hunters and wild animals slaughtered the birds until they were nearly extinct. Today they are protected by conservation laws and are once again increasing.

Hawaii has many colorful native birds: the honeycreeper, the bright yellow mamo, the scarlet iiwi, as well as crows, thrushes, and canaries. Many other birds migrate annually to the islands from their colder native regions. These include the marsh hawk, California gull, Arctic tern, and sandpiper.

The birds that a visitor usually sees in parks or on the roadside are probably not native but imported by the state and private organizations such as the Hui Manu, a society for the protection of birds. These birds are brought in to control insects and to replace other birds that are becoming extinct.

Fertilizing by air is one of many modern methods used by Hawaii's sugar industry.

AGRICULTURE AND INDUSTRY

UP to World War II agriculture was the chief source of livelihood in Hawaii. It centered on two crops, cane sugar and pineapples. After the war, federal military spending became the main source of income. The tourist industry also has overshadowed agriculture in recent years. However, the growing of crops still remains basic to the Hawaiian economy.

The first Hawaiians brought sugarcane with them from Tahiti, and ever since the first successful plantations were started in 1835, it has been the state's leading crop. Ladd and Company on Kauai, started by three New Englanders, was able to export 4,286 pounds of sugar and 2,700 gallons of molasses in 1837. Since then the sugarcane industry has grown into a 200-million-dollar business. In 1965, 1,218,000 tons, or about 11 tons per acre, were produced. Today 236,000 acres of Hawaii's land are planted with sugarcane.

Sugarcane on Hawaii takes two years to grow rather than one year as in other areas, but highly mechanized production methods have put the islands ahead of any competitors in terms of yield per acre.

Pineapples are Hawaii's second leading crop. The state produces about 50 per cent of the world's supply of canned pineapple products and 80 per cent of the nation's supply.

In 1903 James D. Dole set up a simple canning operation on his

Water tank of the Dole Pineapple Company

600-acre pineapple farm, after persuading other farmers in the area to plant the crop. In 1922 the Dole Pineapple Company bought the island of Lanai, and today cultivates over 3,000 of its 90,000 acres in pineapples. Lanai City is a bustling town of 2,400, mostly company employees. From Lanai the pineapples are barged to Honolulu and taken to the Dole cannery in Iwilei. The cannery's 200-foot-tall water tank in the shape of a pineapple is one of the state's tourist attractions.

Hawaii has the largest pineapple canneries in the world. Over 22,000 people work directly for the industry, and many thousands work in related fields. Scientists at the Pineapple Research Institute are constantly experimenting to produce, among other things, a pineapple that will take up less growing room.

Other crops are grown in Hawaii, although not in such large quantities. It is the only state in which coffee is raised, and today it produces about 1 per cent of the world's coffee. Most of the coffee comes from Kona on the island of Hawaii.

Macadamia nuts, a tasty gourmet food, were first brought to the islands in 1890, and today are grown on Maui, Oahu, and Hawaii. Poi, a gray, pastelike food made from the taro plant, was the mainstay of the early Hawaiian diet and is still enjoyed today. Hawaii grows orchids and other flowers for shipment all over the world. Most of the cut flowers are sent to the mainland in the form of *leis* or corsages.

First organized in 1837, livestock raising is a growing Hawaiian industry. Today the state boasts the largest privately owned cattle ranch in the nation. Located in Waimea on Hawaii Island, Parker Ranch has 253,000 acres with more than 42,000 head of Hereford cattle.

But agriculture in Hawaii is now overshadowed by military spending, from which most of the island's money comes. Some 440 million dollars were spent in 1965, in addition to 200 million dollars on related nonmilitary projects.

Since World War II, Hawaii's location as the crossroads of the Pacific has made it the key area in our country's western defenses. And as world interest centers in the Asian countries, Hawaii's importance grows even larger.

The headquarters of the United States Pacific Command, in-

A paniola (Hawaiian cowboy) and his herd in front of a tracking station on Hawaii

Jungle training for the men of Schofield Barracks on Oahu

cluding the Army, Navy, and Air Force, is at Camp H.W. Smith on Oahu. Its purpose is to maintain the security of the Pacific area.

The United States Army of the Pacific, with headquarters at Fort Shafter on Oahu, is geographically the largest army command in the world. Shafter became the nerve center for directing Pacific area operations during World War II. Other Army installations include Schofield Barracks on Oahu, home of the Twenty-fifth Infantry and the largest outpost in the United States; Fort Reuger near Diamond Head, which houses the Hawaii National Guard; Fort Armstrong near Honolulu Harbor, headquarters for the United States Army Engineers; Fort De Russey, the main Armed Forces Rest and Recreational Center for war veterans returning from Pacific area duty.

Of all the military forces the Navy is the largest paymaster in the state, employing 12,500 civilian workers. The Pacific Fleet is based at Pearl Harbor, and consists of 425 ships, 3,000 aircraft, 250,000 sailors, and 76,000 Marines. At Pearl Harbor today are memorials to those who died on December 7, 1941, when the United States was attacked by Japan, and in the harbor itself are the sunken hulls of the warships *Arizona* and *Utah*.

In addition to the Pearl Harbor facilities the Navy maintains a huge shipyard, a submarine base, a supply center, an ammunition depot, an air station, and a base for Polaris submarines.

The United States Marine Corps is located at Camp Smith and the Hawaiian Air Defense Division at Wheeler Air Force Base on Oahu. The Coast Guard patrols an area 1,200 miles east of Hawaii and westward to Asia.

Hawaii's second largest industry is tourism, which the people of Hawaii call the visitor industry. In 1965, tourists contributed 260 million dollars to the state's economy, with over 600,000 visitors coming to the islands, and the number is ever-increasing. From 1955 to 1965 the tourist industry jumped 450 per cent. By 1970 the number of tourists is expected to reach more than a million. Thousands of Hawaiians earn their living directly or indirectly from the

Honolulu waterfront with ocean liner in the background

flow of tourist trade, and this, too, will increase as more and more people discover the delights of this Paradise of the Pacific.

Other industries have boomed within the state. The growth of tourism has brought an increase in the construction business with a high demand for new hotels and apartment houses. The garment industry, also boosted by the increase in tourists, is valued at 22 million dollars a year, and is expected to grow when expensive transportation problems are solved. Hawaii also manufactures scientific and laboratory supplies, cement and cement products, wood, oil, perfume, and musical instruments.

The state has some potential wealth in mineral deposits. Kauai

The Mauna Kea Beach Hotel is a popular attraction.

and Hawaii have large bauxite deposits, of interest to aluminum companies. There is some iron ore but it is difficult to mine, as is the manganese oxide and sulfur. Lava rock is used for art work and as a building material. Reef limestone is used for construction and in the manufacture of lime.

Despite the increasing population and the scarcity of available land, Hawaii's economy is thriving, due mainly to scientific developments, labor and management cooperation, and mechanization. According to the National Industrial Conference Board, the rate of growth of Hawaii is exceeded by only three states and three nations in the world.

Fisherman with his catch of an eel, a fish, and a lobster

HAWAII-A MARINE LABORATORY

EVER since the first Hawaiians set foot on the islands, people have regarded the surrounding waters as a major source of food. There are 584 kinds of fish in Hawaiian waters and most of them are edible. The marine fish range in size from the huge whale shark, some forty to fifty feet long and weighing several tons, to the colorful little damsel fish which measures only a few inches in length. Skipjack tuna is caught and canned at Kewalo Basin in Honolulu and sent all over the world.

Because Hawaii is surrounded by ocean, its people have always been interested in fishing and other water activities. As the population increased, the government found it necessary to regulate fishing and water rights. The first Hawaiians did this by a system of customs and tabus. When the white men came, they used dynamite for killing fish. Although this was outlawed in the early 1900's, the law was not enforced until 1919 when the Fish and Game Commission, now a division of the State Department of Land and Natural Resources, was established. The commission is responsible for fish conservation, operation of fish hatcheries, the introduction and release of fish stocks, and the enforcement of fishing laws.

Many of the brilliantly colored and unusually shaped fish in Hawaiian waters are said to be related to those in the East Indian Ocean. The rose and black moano, the bright blue uku, and the yellow and white kihikihi bear little resemblance to fish found along the west coast of North America or in the seas of Japan.

Visitors can enjoy these fish and many others at the aquarium at Waikiki on Oahu, or at Sea Life Park, an oceanarium containing the largest exhibit of marine life in the world. The oceanarium is part of the Oceanic Institute. The Oceanics Foundation was established in 1960 by Taylor A. Pryor, who conceived of the idea while a graduate student at the University of Hawaii. Sea Life Park opened in 1964 at Makapuu Point on Oahu. One of the institute's outstanding achievements was a project involving Keiki, a trained porpoise. Keiki was released into the open sea and then successfully recalled by underwater electronic sounds.

Federal, state, and private researchers are cooperating in a mas-

Scuba diver and Keiki, the dolphin

Marlin fishing at Kona, Hawaii

sive study of the unknown regions of the sea surrounding Hawaii. These studies call for, among other things, a research submarine to explore the waters.

In 1963 the University of Hawaii initiated the Hawaii Institute of Geophysics (HIG) to handle research projects for the Air Force, National Service Foundation, National Aeronautics and Space Administration, and others. Plans call for an oceanographic research center at Kewalo Basin in Honolulu, a marine life experimental laboratory, and studies of tidal waves and wave forces on beaches. HIG has a marine laboratory on Coconut Island off Oahu for studies of inshore, reef, and bottom fish. Knowledge of the ocean bottom will be put to use in the installation of an underwater tracking station to be used by the Navy for testing equipment and weapons systems.

The HIG, along with private organizations such as the Oceanic Institute and the Bisset-Berman Company, makers of marine science equipment, is working hard to make Hawaii a leading oceanographic research center.

Jets carry passengers between islands.

TRANSPORTATION AND COMMUNICATION

BECAUSE Hawaii is an island state, water transportation has always been of great importance. Today, however, the people of Hawaii are also dependent upon air travel.

Ship transportation in the early days was hazardous. Between 1794 and 1906, 197 vessels were wrecked on Hawaiian shores as a result of storms or navigational errors. Most of the wrecks were at Diamond Head Reef and Waimanalo on the island of Oahu. Today there are lighthouses at both places.

Honolulu is a regular port of call for freight and passenger ships of ten private lines. The Matson Navigation Company is the most important, having dominated Hawaiian shipping since 1930. Other deepwater ports are Nawiliwili and Port Allen on Kauai; Kahului on Maui; and Hilo on Hawaii. In 1902 it took 112 days to sail from New York City to Honolulu. Today ships make the trip to the islands from the west coast of the mainland in four and a half days.

Transportation between the islands has developed from canoes to jet planes. The first steamer, the *Constitution*, was introduced in 1852. In 1883 the Inter-Island Steamship Navigation Company, with eleven vessels, was put into operation. It remained the chief method of transportation between islands until 1950 when the Hawaiian Airlines took over. Today Hawaii is making plans for an island-to-island ferry system.

The first air flight in Hawaii was made in 1911 at Maunalua, Oahu, by Bud Mars. Commander John Rodgers attempted the first flight from the mainland in 1925, but was unsuccessful. Two years later Lieutenants Maitland and Hegenberger made the trip in a trimotor Fokker in twenty-five hours and fifty minutes. Today jet planes reach the fiftieth state in about five hours. In 1935 Pan American began the first commercial air service between the mainland and Hawaii. Other airlines instituted service after World War II. Convenient air travel to the islands has boosted the tourist industry considerably.

Flights between the islands are provided by Hawaiian Airlines, which lands at all airports in the state, and by the Aloha Airlines, which began interisland flights in 1946. A third carrier, Andrews Flying Service, provides unscheduled flights.

Today Hawaii has more airports than seaports. The largest is the International Airport at Honolulu, which replaced the old Rodgers Airport in 1963. Others are at Hilo, Kona, and Kamuela on Hawaii; Molokai and Kalaupapa on Molokai; Kahului, Lahaina, and Hana on Maui; and Lihue on Kauai.

For transportation on the islands themselves Hawaiians used to walk or ride horses. In 1868 the Pioneer Omnibus Line gave Hawaii its first public transportation service. It consisted of two horses and a cart and carried passengers a distance of about two miles for twenty-five cents. The Honolulu Rapid Transit Company, formed in 1901, introduced electric coaches. Since 1957 the city's buses have been diesel hydraulic. Taxis and bus lines provide transportation in the rural districts and on other islands. The first railroad began operating in 1889 but closed down in the 1950's because trucks provided better service. The railroad was the result of the efforts of Benjamin F. Dillingham, and it stimulated the development of sugar and pineapple plantations in rural Oahu.

Only two United States cities — New York and Los Angeles — have more automobile traffic than Honolulu. To solve this common modern-day problem, the state is building a network of freeways on Oahu. To expedite the flow of traffic from Honolulu to wind-

Above, Pali Highway approaching downtown Honolulu; right, traffic in Waikiki

Research station on Mauna Loa

ward Oahu, freeways and two sets of tunnels through the Koolau Mountains were built. These have helped to reduce traffic congestion.

Because water transportation was so slow, communication was very difficult between Hawaii and the mainland before 1902. In that year an underseas cable was completed between San Francisco and the islands. Twin submarine cables were laid in 1957. Radio telephone service has been in operation since 1931. The Hawaiian Telephone Company ranks among the top ten of independent telephone firms in the United States and provides service to 80 per cent of Hawaiian homes. It is the only independent company to serve an entire state.

Hawaii's twenty-five newspapers are printed in English, Japanese, Chinese, Filipino, and Korean. Of the seven daily papers six are in Honolulu and one in Hilo. The largest is the *Honolulu Star-Bulletin*, and the oldest is the *Honolulu Advertiser*, which began in 1856 as the *Pacific Commercial Advertiser*. The state also has twenty-two commercial radio stations and ten television channels. Most of the programs are delayed because the film or tape must be flown from the mainland. However, on November 19, 1966, Hawaii received its first live television broadcast after the satellite *Lani Bird* was launched. Another satellite, now in the planning stage, will provide additional communication circuits for transpacific calls.

Hawaii has also joined the space age. The University of Michigan's Haleakala Observatory is one of the ten largest astronomical observatories in the world and serves as an infrared missile-tracking station. The National Aeronautics and Space Administration is planning an observatory on Mauna Kea, and radar facilities are now in operation on Mount Kaala on Oahu. Hawaii's missile-tracking stations are an important part of America's space program.

Above, remains of temple used by Kamehameha I; left, administration building of East-West Center, University of Hawaii

RELIGION, EDUCATION, AND CULTURE

THE strength of Hawaii lies in the peaceful blending of its people from many different backgrounds. Each has contributed religious and cultural beliefs to the melting pot, and each has benefited from increased educational opportunities.

The early Hawaiians were devoted to four main gods: Kane, god of life; Ku, god of medicine, war, and forests; Lono, god of agriculture, rain, and clouds; and Kaneloa, god of the sea. Religious beliefs were a living part of daily occupations. No project was started without the appropriate religious ceremony.

But by the time the Christian missionaries arrived, the people were without a religion and ready to accept a new one. Queen Kaahumanu had destroyed the idols and temples of the old gods. The missions received help from Hawaii's monarchs, who worked diligently to convert the people to Christianity. In 1824 Queen Kaahumanu issued an edict prohibiting murder, theft, boxing, and work or play on the Sabbath.

A French Catholic colony was established in Hawaii in 1828 by Father Alexis Bachelot, but the Protestants became concerned over the success of the colony and urged the queen to prohibit Catholicism in Hawaii. By 1831 the priests were expelled. However, five years later, an American priest, Father Walsh, was allowed to stay in the islands on condition that he convert foreigners only. Later,

Catholics were guaranteed the same rights and privileges as the Protestant faiths. In 1840 the constitution included a statement on religious tolerance. The Catholic missions in Hawaii established a school to train teachers and to print books, and by 1844 there were three thousand students in one hundred Catholic schools throughout the islands. Today there are over fifteen thousand students in thirty-six schools, including Chaminade College.

Other groups took root in the islands after the 1840 constitution. The Anglican Church was established in 1862. Iolani School for boys was organized that year, and St. Andrews School for girls a year later.

The Latter-Day Saints arrived in 1850 and settled in Laie, Oahu. Over the years they built a Mormon Temple and several tabernacles and established the Church College of the Pacific in 1958. The Hawaiian Mission Academy in Honolulu belongs to the Seventh-Day Adventists, who came to the islands in 1885. The Honpa Hongwanji Mission School, established in 1918, is one of six Buddhist sects in Hawaii.

The religion of the people was always closely tied to education. According to the religious tabus of the early Hawaiians, chiefs were trained to prepare them for their high places in society and commoners were trained for menial labor. Formal education was considered unnecessary; boys learned their fathers' occupations; girls were taught household duties.

The missionaries believed that formal schooling was necessary in order to teach the people to read the Bible. The first school was established at Kailua, Hawaii, with King Liholiho and his queen as pupils. Soon the chiefs were able to read and write, and they gave orders for all adults to learn. By 1832, 40 per cent of the population was in school, and about 85,000 people could read. But very few of these were children.

After 1832 school attendance declined as a result of a teacher shortage and opposition by white men who feared the political influence of the missionaries. Nevertheless, new schools were established: the Lahainaluna School on Maui to train teachers; the Royal School in Honolulu to teach children of chiefs or half-whites; the Oahu Charity School, including children from the Russian settlement of Kamchatka; and such Protestant schools as Wailuku Seminary for Girls and Hilo Boarding School. Punahou School was founded in 1841 to educate missionary children. Today it is one of the largest private preparatory schools west of the Rockies. Bernice Pauahi Bishop, a descendant of Kamehameha I, established the Kamehameha Schools in 1887 for children of Hawaiian descent. These schools have contributed many outstanding leaders to the state.

In 1837 Horace Mann established in Massachusetts the first state-controlled school system in the United States. Three years later Hawaii passed laws for a statewide educational system, making it one of the oldest in the nation. In 1844 the islands passed a compulsory school law based upon the American system of education as practiced in New England. English replaced Hawaiian as the main language in the schools.

In Hawaii today, over 165,000 children attend 211 schools, including 11 special schools for the handicapped. Adults in Hawaii have not lost their interest in education either, as evidenced by the more than 27,000 who attend the many public adult community schools. Hawaii also has 50 private and public technical and trade schools, as well as one university, four colleges (the newest is Hawaii Loa which opened in 1967), and several junior colleges.

The only tax-supported institution of higher learning is the University of Hawaii in Honolulu. Established as a land-grant college in 1907, it was known as the College of Agriculture and Mechanics. In 1920 it became the University of Hawaii, and today its faculty numbers over eleven hundred.

Taking advantage of Hawaii's location, the university has instituted programs that have drawn students from all over the world. Two of these programs are the Pineapple Research Institute and the Coconut Island Marine Laboratory. The university has been

Getting ready for a day of surfing

outstanding in the research of the languages and cultures of Pacific countries. In 1960 Congress established the Center for Cultural and Technical Interchange Between East and West. This institution does not give degrees, but concentrates upon the exchange of students.

The first Hawaiians brought surf riding and the hula dance to the islands. The missionaries brought many of their customs with them, as did all the later groups. All of the people participate in such activities as Aloha Week (Hawaiian); the Cherry Blossom Festival (Japanese); the Narcissus Festival (Chinese); and the Filipino-American Good Will Week. Perhaps the blending of cultures is most evident at a typical island party where the visitor might wear Hawaiian clothes (*mumuu* or *aloha shirt*), and eat *kalua* (meaning "cooked in an underground oven") pig, *sashimi* (Japanese raw-fish salad); *Kim chee* (Korean pickled cabbage relish); *Wun tun min* (Chinese noodles with pork dumplings); *Adobo* (Filipino fried chicken); and American roast ham or turkey.

Hawaiians also enjoy the Honolulu Symphony Orchestra, the Honolulu Theater for Youth, the Bishop Museum, Honolulu Academy of Arts, Kilohana Planetarium, the Community Theater, and many other such centers.

Crossroads of the Pacific, or Gateway to the United States, this fiftieth state in the Union is unmatched in the beauty of its land and the warmth of its people.

GLOSSARY

alii — ah-*lee*-ee
Haleakala — hah-lay-*ah*-kah-*lah*
hau — hah-oo
hiiloa — hee-ee-*low*-ah
Hilo — *hee*-low
Hui Manu — hoo-ee *mah*-noo
iiwi — ee-*ee*-vee
ilio — ee-*lee*-oh
Iolani — *ee*-oh-la-nee
Iwilei — ee-vee-*lay*
Kaahumanu — kah-*ah*-hoo-*mah*-noo
Kaala — kah-*ah*-lah
Kahoolawe — kah-*hoh*-oh-*lah*-vay
Kahului — kah-oo-*loo*-ee
Kalakaua — kah-*lah*-*kah*-oo-ah
Kalanianaole — kah-*lah*-ne-ah-*nah*-o-lee
Kalaupapa — kah-*lah*-oo-*pah*-pah
Kalihi — kah-*lee*-hee
kalua — kah-loo-ah
Kamehameha — kah-*may*-hah-*may*-hah
Kamuela — kah-moo-*ell*-lah
Kaneohe — kah-nay-*oh*-hay
Kauai — kah-oo-ah-*ee*
Kealakekua — kay-ah-*lah*-kay-koo-ah
Keiki — kah-*ee*-kee
kihikihi — *kee*-hee-*kee*-hee
Kilohana — kee-loh-*hah*-nah
kokea — koh-*kay*-ah
kou — *koh*-oo
kuhina-nui — koo-*hee*-nah-noo-*ee*
kukui — koo-*koo*-ee
Kure — *koo*-ray
Lanai — lah-*nah*-ee
laukahi — lah-oo-*kah*-hee
Liholiho — *lee*-hoh-lee-hoh
Liliuokalani — lee-*lee*-oo-oh-kah-*lah*-nee
Lunalilo — *loo*-nah-*lee*-loh
Mahele — mah-*hay*-lee
Makapuu — *mah*-kah-*poo*-oo
mamo — mah-*moh*
Maui — *mau*-ee
Mauna Kea — *mau*-nah-*kay*-ah
Mauna Loa — *mau*-nah-*loh*-ah
Maunalua — *mau*-nah-*loo*-ah
moa — *mo*-ah
moano — moh-*ah*-no
Molokai — moh-loh-*kah*-ee
Nawiliwili — nah-*wee*-lee-*wee*-lee
nene — *nay*-nay
Nihoa — nee-*hoh*-ah
Niihau — nee-ee-*hah*-oo
noni — *noh*-nee
Oahu — oh-*ah*-hoo
ohia — oh-*hee*-ah
palapala — *pah*-lah-*pah*-lah
poha — poh-*hah*
popolu — poh-*poh*-loo
puaa — poo-*ah*-ah
uku — *oo*-koo
Waialeale — *wy*-ah-lee-*ah*-lee
Wailuku — wy-*loo*-koo
Waimea — wy-*may*-ah

BIBLIOGRAPHY

Books

Allen, Riley H. *The Story of Hawaii's Flag.* Honolulu: Honolulu Star-Bulletin Publishing Co., 1961.

Armitage, George P., and Judd, Henry P. *Ghost Dog and Other Hawaiian Legends.* Honolulu: Advertiser Publishing Co., 1944.

Bishop National Bank. *Biological Sketches of Hawaii's Rulers.* Honolulu: Bishop Museum Press, 1959.

Boswell, Douglas. *Thrum's Hawaii Annual, Volume 88: All About Hawaii.* Honolulu: Honolulu Star-Bulletin Publishing Co., 1966.

Elder, Nell B. *Pineapple in Hawaii.* Honolulu: Advertiser Publishing Co., 1961.

Eskridge, Robert L. *Umi, The Hawaiian Boy Who Became King.* Chicago: J. C. Winston Co., 1936.

Fulloway, David, and Krauss, Noel L. H. *Common Insects of Hawaii.* Honolulu: Tongg Publishing Co., 1945.

Gosline, William, and Brock, Vernon. *Handbook of Hawaiian Fishes.* Honolulu: University of Hawaii Press, 1960.

Henshaw, H. W. *Birds of the Hawaiian Islands.* Honolulu: T. G. Thrum Publishing Co., 1902.

Judd, Henry P. *The Hawaiian Language.* Honolulu: Honolulu Star-Bulletin Publishing Co., 1919.

Kuck, Lorraine E., and Tongg, Richard C. *Hawaiian Flowers.* Honolulu: Tongg Publishing Co., 1943.

———. *Hawaiian Flowers and Flowering Trees.* Honolulu: Tongg Publishing Co., 1960.

Lind, Andrew W. *Hawaii's Japanese, an Experiment in Democracy.* Princeton: Princeton University Press, 1946.

Mellon, Kathleen. *Hawaiian Heritage.* New York: Hastings House Publishers, Inc., 1963.

Munroe, George C. *Birds of Hawaii.* Honolulu: Tongg Publishing Co., 1944.

Potter, Norris W., and Kasdon, Lawrence M. *Hawaii, Our Island State.* Columbus: Charles E. Merrill Books Inc., 1964.

Taylor, Clarice B. *Hawaiian Almanac.* Honolulu: Tongg Publishing Co., 1957.

Tinker, Spencer W. *Hawaiian Fishes.* Honolulu: Tongg Publishing Co. 1944.

Wist, Benjamin O. *A Century of Public Education in Hawaii.* Honolulu: Honolulu Star-Bulletin Publishing Co., 1940.

Yzendoorn, Father Reginald, S.S.C.C. *History of the Catholic Mission in Hawaii.* Honolulu: Honolulu Star-Bulletin Publishing Co., 1927.

Reports
Bank of Hawaii, Department of Business Research, 1966.
B. P. Bishop Museum, 1957, 1963, 1964.
City and County of Honolulu, "Mayor's Report," 1965; "Board of Water Supply," 1958-64.
Hawaiian Historical Society, 1958-64.
State Department of Agriculture, 1964, 1966.
State Department of Education, 1963-64; 1965-66.
State Department of Land and Natural Resources, Division of Fish and Game, 1962-65.
State Department of Planning and Economic Development, 1963-66.

Periodicals and Newspapers
"Fountain of Fire in Hawaii," *National Geographic Magazine,* March, 1960; "Hawaii, U.S.A.," July, 1960.
"Hawaii," *Life,* October 8, 1965.
"Hawaii," *Time,* December 16, 1966.
"Hawaii, Taps at Pearl Harbor," *Saturday Evening Post,* December 17, 1966.
"Hawaiian Rip Tide," *Vogue,* November, 1966.

Hawaii Schools, official bulletin, Department of Education.
Honolulu Advertiser, 1959-66.
Honolulu Star-Bulletin, 1963-66.
Paradise of the Pacific Magazine, annual Christmas issues, 1942-64.

INDEX